W0019589
9781659825978

Access the free Video Course Companion at:

https://course.innodemia.com/p/101-tips-for-effective-product-managers/

Paolo Messina and Michael Fox respond live to over 15 product management questions from a world wide audience of product managers .

101 Tips for Effective Product Managers

Product management is one of the most idealized, desired and publicized business roles in the tech industry (as well as many other industries). Scores of students, engineers and professionals in business operations, sales and marketing dream of becoming a Product Manager.

Much has been written about how to get a job in this profession and how to think about the strategic parts of the job. Furthermore, there are dozens of trainings online that can help with curating a roadmap, making products that people love and interacting with customers. Much less is said about the day-to-day challenges you will find when starting your career in product management.

The purpose of this book is not to be the perfect or exhaustive guide to product management. Rather, our aim is to take an employee beginning their career and give 101 practical pieces of knowledge which will help him or her with the day-to-day reality of the job.

In particular, this book was written for those facing practical challenges in product management, including product managers working in small and medium-sized organizations. Organizations where product managers will have limited budgets, limited time and an overarching need for fast, practical knowledge which will help them immediately.

Here are 101 practical tips that will help you do the job (and also get the job, too) and avoid complications!

These tips are not meant to be an exhaustive coverage of product management best practices, nor can they work with absolute precision in each case.

Some current product managers may also have different views and may not agree with these tips and notes. Some may feel that one shouldn't discuss the practical portions of the job without also discussing the strategic. It is our opinion that practical discussion is needed more than ever before. With the adoption of Agile methods for software development, digital manufacturing and data science, Product Management is now as much about strategy as it is practical day-to-day activities which organize strategy into execution.

Our 101 Tips for Effective Product Managers represent a body of insights gained on real projects (over 20 combined years in product management plus 15 years in R&D), the interaction with 50+ (Silicon Valley and beyond) product managers, as well as from the study of over 100 books in product management, marketing, persuasion and general management, product development, and innovations that several professionals may find helpful and handy. Both of us also each hold multiple graduate degrees.

In addition, this book was reviewed by 10 product managers with a combined 100+ years of experience from around the world.

The style is schematic, and it is meant to provide quick access to key insights without dwelling on excessive conceptual elaboration. The book is not intended to be read sequentially; refer to the table of contents to find the relevant tips for your particular situation. Each section starts with an opening that is meant to help visualize the practical situation.

Expert's insights

About the Authors

Paolo Messina is a Product Manager and Entrepreneur. During the last several years he has worked at B2B SAAS (software as a service) companies as well as B2C internet companies. He has worked on Web, Mobile, Integrated apps and Digital Information products. He also worked on platforms operations focusing on both improving operational experience as well as leveraging artificial intelligence to improve user interfaces. His current focus is in Artificial Intelligence (A.I.) powered products. He consulted for several startups in silicon valley, such as the Augmented Reality pioneer Looksery before it became Snapchat visual effects. He has also consulted with IOT and merging A.I. powered industrial and consumer devices companies. He is the founder of Innodemia, a company that helps managers, product managers, Intrapreneurs, innovators and entrepreneurs to learn building insanely good A.I. products and processes.

Michael Fox has most recently held leadership roles in Product, Offering Development, Presales, Design and Technical Publications. In earlier parts of his career he worked as a startup founder and in leading technical operations for SaaS companies. For the last 10 years he has worked as an "Intrapreneur" on more than 8 different initiatives in public and private companies ranging in size from $350M to $24B. These initiatives spanned the world of technology in areas such as consulting, developing complex B2B solutions, building new products, expanding to new markets, executing joint ventures and developing new alliances.

Table of Contents

Product Management Top Highlights

Context:

The product manager spends a considerable amount of time defining market problems and product features, as well as discussing, iterating, and at times, debating with engineers and designers.

The Most Critical To-Dos

1 Focus on understanding user, buyer behavior and value drivers. Develop a profound empathy for the customer. Walk through the full steps a customer walks through to acquire the product. These are often captured in journey maps which include an overlay of empathy. Simulate this journey to the best of your ability, or better yet, go through the journey yourself (if B2C) or with sales (if B2B). Interact with and deeply understand the sales process, buy the product, go through the delivery (or shipment), experience the thrill to open the package when it arrives (or log in if it is a software product). Interact with the customer support to solve a problem you have encountered or a question you have. Understand how the customer feels and how pleasant or painful the support process is. Repeat this experience multiple times a year.

2 Double check quality control: do not assume engineering and/or Q&A do it right. Exceptions may include very early-stage product tests and situations where the test plan cannot forecast the actual ways and patterns the users will exploit your product.

3 Avoid direct conflicts, especially with engineering. When confronted with opposition, take time to ask advice from peers and super-

Paolo Messina and Michael Fox

visors and to design a proper communication strategy[1]. The ultimate job of a product manager is to make the product and business successful. This cannot be done if conflicts exist with Engineering, Sales, Marketing or other parties.

4   Be a very good marketer: aspire to master persuasion like a salesperson! Understand the ultimate value to the customers and to the company of the organization's strategy, and align your roadmap to the strategy. Ensure you understand the way your product is found within its market and the numerous stages of the sales cycle (sales journey) of your product.

5   Understand the system engineering of your products better than the engineers, if possible.

Critical Not-To-Dos

6   Do not blindly believe the Pareto principle (80/20 rule) for use cases in every circumstance. Investigate deeply if there is a need to support use cases for the 20% in the early stages. For example, you may decide to eliminate a feature and discover later that you have alienated an important customer segment. Therefore, your product retention goes down and/or your sales teams receive major complaints.

---

[1]   It seems obvious, but we wanted to make sure you are clear you also avoid conflicts with customers.

7 Avoid the fallacy of thinking that only a very tiny percentage of users may be impacted. Sometimes this is equivalent to saying "Only 10,000 people will die; we have 350 million people, so 10,000 is a small number". Put yourself in the shoes of those 10,000 people: would you like such an outcome?

8 Do not override existing processes or specs without understanding the ramifications. You could kill a feature that is important for a group of customers or a process that was put in place to hack some bug (which obviously will come back!).

9 Do not launch anything without proper testing. You may design fast experiments on a very small scale but when you launch even a beta version at a relevant scale, testing is crucial.

Understanding Your Business Context

Keeping track of where your company is in the following table will help prioritize tasks and understand the major business expectations. Many possible combinations exist, and we invite you to research cases for each. Here are a few pics to give you an idea:

Business Model	Company Size			
	STARTUP	SMB	LARGE	VERY LARGE
B2B		⊘		
B2C				
B2SMB				

⊘ *Usually SMBs have limited cash resources and cannot invest in excessive specialization. You will find that QA, Design, Engineering and Marketing tend to have a matrix organization. The same person follows multiple projects, so be mindful of your requests to a non-specialized, very busy workforce*

Understanding where your company is in its life stage (inception, growth, maturity, decline) will help you to form the proper expectations for you and your product. Attend "All Hands Meetings" and read financial reports. If you work in a public enterprise, ensure you read 10Ks, 10Qs, and other SEC filings about your company. Pay particular attention to the cash, income, marketing expenses, R&D expenses and debt numbers

Business Model	Company Size			
	STARTUP	GROWTH	MATURITY	DECLINE
B2B				
B2C			⚠️	
B2SMB				

⚠️ *Usually these companies will have substantial cash reserves, a solid brand and a high level of specialization per product line. Your work may be very specific, for example: a component of a consumer product or a component of a process within the company operations. Expect lengthy and structured processes; understand you are part of a larger puzzle. Understand who are the key influencers with which you need to work. These companies are looking for growth opportunities. They have the resources and cash to invest, but winning these resources requires substantial research and selling work.*

Understanding where your product is with respect to the marketing maturity and market dynamic will also clarify how to make decisions. Paolo discusses this at length in his courses[2], but here is a table that can help you visualize the proper variables to look into. An overview:

Market Maturity	Product Life			
	RESEARCH	ABOUT TO LAUNCH	POST LAUNCH	MATURE
Emerging Market			@	
Mature Market				
Declining Market				

@ *This could be the case of a growth SaaS service or a Growth Consumer company. They may be a startup or a product within an established company. At this point the product market fit is achieved and the goal is to grow. Growth means increasing customers, increasing product usage, retaining customers and growing revenue. Lots of company and product efforts will be focused on this. These companies are very focused on the goal and have very little latitude for other initiatives... For example, proposing an entirely new product at this stage may not be well received. Analyzing the data to discover the drivers of customer retention may be a great initiative on your side. Retention is crucial to fuel growth. Another example to continue growth could be to consider extending the product to an adjacent market, such as moving up the value chain by tackling several simple use cases.*

---

2   Check course.innodemia.com

Paolo Messina and Michael Fox

Product Research

Context:

The product manager spends a considerable amount of time understanding customers to design new products or services and/or improve existing products and services

10 Data only reveals so much; do not solely rely on it. Especially in Internet companies, data becomes a credo. Quantitative data collected digitally can reveal existing behaviors. Qualitative data collected in open-ended questions reveals the "why" behind these behaviors. Knowing the "why" leads to unexpected recipes to improve the product.

11 People cannot always articulate the details of what they need, but always try to know what they would do. Observe their behavioral patterns as much as you can.

12 Design experiments that lead to measurable quantities. Fast experimentation is preferable but not always possible. Optimizing copy and font size can be feasible. Changing complex back-end operations are much more difficult to experiment with. In complex B2B products, experimentation may take weeks because it can be difficult to access users and customers.

13 Research deeply the processes and the tactics needed to market and launch a product. These aspects will likely impact the chances for success and will also inform compromises and feature prioritization. For example, there is likely no reason to spend four months on a feature that customers will experience only two months into the use of the product. There are many other adoption barriers that could be tackled first.

14 Find and exploit creative ways to leverage existing data. For example, Google search trends can offer many insights on how consumers and prospects perceive a problem, topic, and/or product category, and how they approach the category.

15 Create venues to collect insights on a regular basis. You can collect suggestions, problems and ideas from[3]:

- Customer support personnel
- Customer support tickets
- Sales professionals (including sales engineers)
- Account managers
- Everyone in the company who is also a user or is close to the end customer

---

[3] Collecting indirect insights from various groups is not a substitute for your direct relationship with customers.

Paolo Messina and Michael Fox

Get The Basics Right

Context:

Before you embark on the most sophisticated areas of product management, make sure you know how to define the basic objectives of the user experience.

16 Focus on the basic needs when making requirements, and capture these in design flows.

17 Understand superfluous steps in your user flow, e.g. you have a flow made of three steps A->C->B (from A to C and from C to B) . Can you have the user go directly from A->B and spare the user one superfluous step?

18 How does the customer go from A->B (step A to step B)? How do customers go back from B->A (step B to step A)? Make sure you think through the reverse user flow.

19 What happens if while going from A->B the customer does something not forecasted, or something else happens? Exception behaviour must be analyzed and defined in detail.

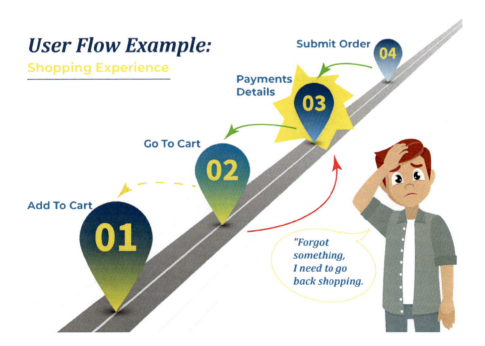

User Flow Example:
Shopping Experience

Submit Order — 04
Payments Details — 03
Go To Cart — 02
Add To Cart — 01

"Forgot something, I need to go back shopping.

Product Design

Context:

A product manager works constantly with designers and user experience researchers.

20 Do not tell the designers and engineers what the solution should be; highlight the problem or benefit you want to achieve. Let designers be accountable for design and engineers for how the technical problem is solved.

21 Explain why a problem or benefit is so crucial to the success of the product. Explain the relative hierarchy of problems and benefits so the team is clear on priorities.

22 Show examples of solutions to your designers. Point out that you are doing so only in the interest of explaining the need and better visualizing what is in your mind. Your designers are free to re-interpret the design as long as they solve the customer need or business objective.

23 Be picky on the visual design, look and feel. Require that tests are conducted. If in a small company, organize lunches and have your company employees that are not familiar with the product design process provide feedback (or conduct hallway tests). The feedback may be biased (they likely want to maintain good relationships and do not want to offend you) but it is helpful to get started.

24 Help your design team research useful best practices including scientific literature on design, behavior and best practices. This is an area where a lot of academic research is available in decision science and should be leveraged as much as necessary in your product design. Google Scholar is a good place to start.

Paolo Messina and Michael Fox

Persuading Engineers

Context:

The relationship with engineers is the bread and butter of product management, especially in the early years of your career. In order to effectively collaborate with engineers, you should know and understand their world and lingo. This doesn't mean you need to be a programmer yourself. Yet, the better technological understanding and knowledge you have, the better and more effective your collaboration with the engineers will be.

Paolo Messina and Michael Fox

25 Understand where the engineer is in his journey with the company:

- Do they like the job? Are they frustrated with the work at hand?

- Do they have issues such as performance, etc?

- Do they have expectations of being promoted? Is what you are asking placing their promotion at risk?

- Are they eager to learn more or have an impact?

- Do they feel they could contribute more?

- Do you understand how you can phrase your communication better to convince engineers working towards the business objectives?

26 Offer sincere appreciation of their work, pointing out aspects you can honestly and genuinely appreciate. It can be risky and it is not an industry-accepted practice, however we feel asking engineers for feedback on design increases their personal investment in the project.

27 Present new ideas to show how they could be great for the company but also help them achieve one of their goals (see above) or mitigate a problem they are experiencing.

28 Understand that the responsibility to deliver rests with the engineer. When they feel responsible, they instinctively trigger their fear to fail. Find a way to alleviate the fear of failure to prevent objections based on fear more than on merit.

29 Listen to their feedback carefully and ask more questions. Do not be afraid of saying you do not know something. An engineer prefers to explain than have a pretentious product manager create more problems by remaining ignorant.

30 Do your research, including technical research, so you can identify areas where the team should acquire knowledge. This will help you provide added value to engineers.

Do your research

31 Provide value by illustrating your knowledge of the end-to-end system engineering and use cases. Engineers usually work on specific tasks and tend to lose the overview of the full system, especially if it is in the early stages of their career. Bring in information from which they can learn and tell stories that make them feel part of building something valuable.

32 Share the glory of a launch or a mention or compliment you've received from executives with engineers. This is very important as you need to give visibility to their hard and very often obscure work. Give up your ego. Don't be the product manager that just launched the product, and instead lavishly praise each and every engineer and scientist on the team that contributed to this.

33 If there is a strong difference in opinions you may need to confront an engineer. You may go to their supervisor, but we do not recommend complaining. Sometimes it is better to face the situation directly. Approach them as if you are detecting a difference in behavior or performance. In this way you ensure the conflict is between the engineer's current self and their past self rather than between you and them. Chances are this person will then make the necessary adjustments themselves to return to their previously earned status.

Providing Requirements to Engineers, Designers and Other Stakeholders

Context:

Providing written requirements for what needs to be built (or not) is a crucial part of product management.

34 First, explain the "why" at a high level using a presentation, storyboard, mockup or a brief (not a book) user story.

35 Reiterate the "why" at each and every possible occasion, especially in small talks during the scrum or when you have a blackboard session. Most people know "how" but not "why". The "why" is the driver.

36 If you decide to add new tickets to your task management software, discuss them in person with the person or group that will execute them. It is often helpful to schedule regular grooming sessions to have time reserved for these discussions. Discuss constraints and boundaries of your new request in advance whenever possible. This is also known as pre-framing so that your counterpart is ready to receive the new task and does not perceive it as a surprise.

Paolo Messina and Michael Fox

37 The ticket must be effective and easy to read; avoid writing a poem about the user story. Tell the big "why" in the initial communication discussed above.

38 The specific requirement should contain:

- ○ Concise context explanation
- ○ An accurate description of the functions/flows you are requesting (see above for how this should be designed)
- ○ A list of things you do not want to happen, risks that should be minimized, and qualifiers for performances (of which acceptance criteria are an example; in platforms these could be operations load min/max, frequency, precision, accuracy, whether asynchronous is acceptable, etc.)

39 For complex projects or requirements go back and talk to the engineers one-on-one to make sure they understand correctly and have a specific avenue to express concern or request modifications. This is the best way misunderstandings are avoided. This is often time-consuming and cannot always be done, but should be done before the most important or complex tickets. Some people in the industry call this "radical alignment".

Training Sales and Marketing Teams

Context:

Providing training to product marketing, sales teams and support teams is a crucial product management task. Depending on the company, it can be done at the time of major product launches or major features launch.

40 With B2B products, take this very, very seriously. Product success depends on properly training the sales team. This is also very relevant in high ticket (cost $1K or more) B2C models where inside sales teams make the final sale.

41 Usually, marketing will organize the "how" and "when" to teach the sales team, but you need to prepare the material. Invest the time necessary to produce high-quality material. Partner with marketing if you need videos or more stylish presentations. This is often given the term "sales enablement."

42 The training goal is to bring the sales and support teams up to speed with market problems, product value and features. This is crucial for them to become product experts in their sales and/or support process. Another training goal is to provide a long-term plan to marketing. Marketing will refine the message and keep the sales team up to speed, train new sales personnel and produce all the necessary communication for customers.

43 Chat with sales in advance. Have 1-3 close relationships who will act as your insiders that honestly tell you about concerns, customer feedback, product shortcomings, and competitive pressure.

44 Do not start from product features, even in established markets with mature products. Set the stage of what new experience/new capabilities your customers are now able to access and why this is important.

45 Create a venue where every week or two, marketing, sales and support can be informed of what is happening in the product. They all need to know about this to prepare their own work. Issue release notes to make sure these teams have a place to read and review. You should always proactively inform these teams prior to releases.

46 DO NOT TALK about new features until they are very advanced or near to feature release. Marketing and sales teams are lovely people and like to talk; that is why they will sell the new feature before you have it. Do not mention new features until they have been through beta testing to avoid misunderstandings and find your next feature already being widely sold to your company's customers!

Vision and Strategy

Context:

Product managers understand the company strategy and develop a roadmap to execute it. At the same time they inform the company strategy by making proposals and conveying the results of their research. In B2C or digital SaaS companies, product managers often take a larger role in the company strategy.

47 It is necessary to fully and completely understand the company strategy as this will drive a portion of your road-map and its item's prioritization (the market driving much of the rest of the roadmap). The strategy also informs on how to communicate product vision to engineers and sales teams. We believe the product manager is like a relay broadcast station (in larger companies with top down strategy): she or he will have to re-phrase, re-frame and clarify the strategy for the target audience.

48 Whoever you report to is likely to have more direct access to those who make the strategy. Try to get as much information as possible from this person. This will also let you know how this person is held accountable and how they are measured, which is often critical in understanding their priorities and how they align to the corporate strategy.

49 Double - check your understanding of company strategy with other PM peers; they have probably picked up an angle or an insight you may have missed.

Double-check

50 In companies that allow for bottom up innovation, (a product is conceived prototyped and tested by small teams), there is a lot more fun! You can actually come up with a product strategy. In order to do this, you need to have very good relationships with marketing, sales, and support as they can inform you about the current market status.

51 Product strategy cannot only be dictated from insights gained in secondary research. By interviewing your colleagues and/or acquiring data on customers, you can use primary research to contribute to your product strategy. There are various models from the "job to be done", the "lead user model", and the "business model generation canvas". Paolo discusses this in his courses, and it is a pretty vast topic.

52 To form an effective strategy, one needs to understand what trends will emerge in the next 1-5 years and from there, understand how your current or future products could catch one of these trends and satisfy an emerging need.

53 Disruptive or pioneering innovation is an altogether different beast (think Elon Musk or Alfred Mann). All sizable companies should have a portfolio of different product initiatives, including the crazy ones. Many people judge innovation in terms of expected ROI, but it is also important to consider optionality. Disruptive innovation brings learning, in-house experts, and lots of morale and enthusiasm, even if it fails.

Selling projects to executives

Context:

It is often said that product managers do not have much authority, since nobody reports into them. Part of this can be true, but it is important to remember that executives are in desperate need of ideas and sources of organic growth. Oftentimes, enormous internal sales efforts are required to build and launch new projects and initiatives. Here is an example of what Paolo learned from raising over $1M at Walmart Labs.

54 You need a champion, someone who has been in the organization longer than you, has enough connections, and has something to gain from a specific project. This person may be your internal customer, the person that has the problem, or a person with a problem that your proposed innovation will solve. Ideally this person is a trusted advisor to one or more executive sponsors.

Find a champion

55 Help your champion showcase that a solution exists to the problem. If possible, show that the solution costs much less in the long term and that the only mistake the company could make is not investing in this!

What if you are developing a new consumer product? Well, it could be there is a VP of engineering that for years wanted to do something and that something can be incorporated by your product. Or, there is a marketing executive who has bet their career on a certain trend and your product would try to catch that trend. These are potential allies[4].

56 How do you find your champion? Dedicate time to network: reach out to more people and become known in the organization. This is like your own personal word-of-mouth marketing. Reading books on attraction marketing will help, too.

57 You can also use the approach to "ask for authority". In this approach you ask for 30-45 minutes to make a presentation on an important issue, e.g. too much product inventory or product adoption too sluggish. In the presentation, you identify that the lack of a centralized point of authority causes a situation where the company is losing money or missing opportunities. Basically you make your audience problem aware and ask for the authority to rectify the situation.

---

[4] Even if they are higher in the hierarchy, it does not matter if you solve their problem or satisfy their passion. This is your internal customer. They will eventually make the sale you need to produce all the marketing material to support the sale!

Partnering With Other PMs

In the early stages of your career and particularly when you are in a large company, you will be part of a team of peer product managers (PMs). They are also stakeholders and can be your best allies or your worst detractors. Recognize right away they are important stakeholders. The specifics depend on a case by case situation and whether or not your product overlaps consistently with other PMs' products as well as how the organization is staffed with engineering and marketing.

58 If you succeed in establishing good relationships with engineers and scientists, they naturally, by virtue of the fact they are human beings, will tend to favor your tickets over those of other product managers. When working with shared resources, avoid having your share of resources be too predominant by trying to get a closer understanding of the day-to-day workload and coordinating work with other product managers.

59 Try to coordinate your work with that of other product managers. Sometimes you can organize joint scrum sessions to better align the team's work. Identify 2 or 3 PMs with which you can build strong relationships. This will help you both keep up-to-date with informal news and keep you further along your roadmap.

60 Even if the product management team roadmap is agreed to quarterly, the actu al execution will inevitably result in variations and competition for resources. Take time to review your backlog and re-prioritize tickets as necessary.

61 Explain to your colleagues when you make changes in prioritization which favor their needs, as this could eventually bring some goodwill and they will be willing to do the same when you need it.

62 Try to be helpful and resourceful for others: it will expose you to new challenges, expand your network, and give you experience.

63 Reach out to PMs in other organizations and around the world, with different cultures, business models and industries to keep learning from real case scenarios.

R&D and Radical Innovation

Context:

Management of R&D requires a book all of its own. R&D is often of two different natures, either incremental or disruptive. It can be more scientific in nature or more engineering-focused. The type of R&D companies conduct changes from industry to industry and from company to company. The biotech sector is very scientifically driven, whereas other sectors focus solely on engineering development. If you work in digital and internet products you will be in touch with the artificial intelligence movement. This sector is a hybrid: some projects staff scientists and can be focused to apply academic research; other projects are closer to product development. Here are some tips:

64 You need to help scientists work on stuff that interests them and that is potentially useful, including your project. Scientists usually come from academia and, while they share traits in common with engineers, they are used to working on stuff they enjoy. Many cannot live without this.

65 Take part in R&D meetings, brainstormings, and presentations whenever possible to strengthen relationships and understand what is happening. This will help formulate requirements and product strategy if you are working on a highly R&D driven project. You can also take part in meetings making presentations on trends in the industry and applications that are interesting for monetization. This is a simple yet effective way to promote innovation and develop mutually beneficial relationships.

66 Be a salesperson for innovative R&D projects within your organization. In large companies, enough money is available to dedicate part of the daily activities or the personnel to R&D. You need to continually remind engineering and product leadership that these projects are important and have both direct and indirect benefits (i.e. know how, morale, retention).

67 You need to be able to drive R&D towards monetization. The key difference between research in academia and in companies is that in companies, R&D eventually needs to be monetized. A key component of that is to have your team switching from understanding everything to understanding enough to exploit what has been discovered. One way to facilitate this is to create a process for incorporating snippets of new findings, e.g. a new algorithm, into prototypes and test them.

- Create a process for integrating snippets of new findings, e.g. a new algorithm, with existing processes and methods to produce an incremental improvement or test a new benefit.

- Such integration generates data that can further the exploration and development of the original piece of R&D. An example includes modifying or improving an algorithm with real usage data.

68 Incentivize relationships with academia by getting publications in both academic and industry journals, patent applications, conference presentations, blogs, and other social media participation. Scientists and engineers love all of this, so be the champion of their dreamland, but ask for concreteness in exchange. See the point above: they have to finalize the work toward monetization and not get stuck in continuous exploration like in academia.

69 Understand and use the concept of R&D leverage: an incremental result in R&D can lead to a bigger result in business. If done right, this is the process where millions of dollars are created in R&D driven industries. In order to do this right, you must have a "north star", at least one business problem that can drastically benefit from the incremental improvement of R&D.

Product Quality Control

Context:

Ensuring the right product quality is a highly important area of product management. Product quality control is an area not usually discussed in most product management resources (likely because it is not fancy) but it really makes the difference.

70 You need to define basic product KPIs that must be satisfied. Often engineering will say that a work or a feature or even a product is completed and delivered. The challenge is that that feature dependability and error rate may not satisfy basic product requirements. Only by defining these KPIs in advance can you spot these issues early. The further ahead in the release process you spot this, the higher the pain for the company and for yourself.

71 Product management must understand in detail how engineering and operations control quality at the various release levels. If necessary, identify gaps and influence decision makers to review the process. This can be a touchy area because the supervision often falls under a specific manager, but the consequences to ship a bad product are paid both by the product manager and the end customer.

72 Product managers must review test cases very closely and, if necessary, influence modifications. As automation and artificial intelligence become more popular in this sector, paradoxically more problems arise. Although product managers are not testers, it is highly recommended to test major use cases on your own. Do not blindly trust QA.

73 A huge difference exists between a unit test (the test of specific functions in isolation) and a functional[5] test (the test of a flow in real scenarios). The product manager must oversee the functional test and ensure at least the major relevant flows are tested consistently.

74 Quality control cost can quickly become an issue, and applying high standards may mean that the current workforce (even if assisted from automation) is insufficient. This is a problem, especially in startups, small, and medium-sized companies. Unfortunately, the product manager will have to reach a compromise in some cases and prioritize the testing of the major usage patterns (expected usage patterns).

75 Have a plan or process to handle unexpected situations. Be aware that prioritizing the testing of the user flows with the highest expected usage patterns may mean that defects in untested flows cause significant customer frustration. When you are in a hurry or do not have the resources to test uncommon user flows, be aware of the negative impact the defects could have: if you work on a platform that has millions of users, 0.1% of those users is still a big number!

---

[5] If partner interfaces are involved, then it will be difficult to have a complete functional test. Any time a partner is involved, the team must consider additional factors (no internet, credential issue, bad data received, no acknowledgement received, latency, etc.). Provide the user with the best possible outcome and internal alerting rather than presenting a system error and leaving a session or transaction in an unknown state for the user.

101 Tips for Effective Product Managers

Product Launch

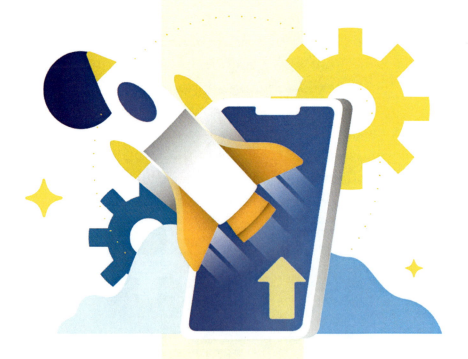

Product launch is one of the most critical elements in product management. It requires planning among many different departments in the company. For complex products which also have an extensive set of resellers, value added resellers, and suppliers it requires coordination with these stakeholders too.

76 Human beings are affected by "priming bias" also simply known as "first impression matters". If you work for an established company, do not launch anything in production without first vetting that it works. In startups, at least in the early stages, depending on the context, you may still favor speed over precision.

77 If it is a first-time launch, make sure you have a measurement system in place both for qualitative and quantitative research. In this phase you need to focus primarily on measuring customer acquisition and activation.

78 If it is a first-time launch, you will need to enroll beta customers early. In an established company, work with marketing to recruit these customers. In a startup, you may have to do everything yourself!

79 Put care into selecting your beta customers. Ideally these should be early adopters that have a strong need or problem to solve. This way you make sure they are really motivated. This is not always possible, so you may have to select customers or prospects that have had a long relationship with your company. The latter will make them more inclined to take

Select the right Beta Customers

the time. Try to select a sample of beta users that tend to use the product in different ways and for different use cases. Make sure to call some of them and have a pre-qualification process so that marketing can help you in qualifying the candidates.

80 You should gain the following information from a beta program:

- Identify experiences that could be improved
- Identify redundant or low value experiences (for the lovers of the minimum viable product (MVP) approach, this step may seem unnecessary, but it is)
- Understand if there are better product configurations / packaging
- Get testimonials and collect user viewpoints, including their expressions, so you can use these in your marketing campaign

81 A beta program, in theory, should not be used for the following. However, sometimes when funding is limited, you have to compromise (if you do, know that you lose all the marketing goodwill that comes free with having free beta customers):

- Load test, engineering endurance, and fatigue tests
- Overall user flow test
- Bug finding

82 Launching can also be interpreted as launching a single feature or process in a large established internet company. In my experience, I recommend the following steps if the change has the potential to impact revenue or other processes:

- Identify a specific subset of the experience or of the user population to which you will launch first

- Identify all the stakeholders and gain their acceptance and trust

- Have a clear revision and reverse plan, that will both help avoid disasters and win consensus

- Identify, with your stakeholders, the best time for the launch as well as a time window in case this is a test

- Design a measurement approach that will clearly identify the qualitative results of the product launch at a minimum (Quantitative is better: Did conversion improve? Did engagement improve? Did error rate decrease?)

83 If you are launching a completely new product, or you are in a startup setting trying to launch a product for the first time, there is a specific marketing strategy known as "Product Launch" that can be followed. There is an abundance of literature on this subject, but here are some of the main steps to retain:

- Identify an audience, and get in touch with this audience with 3-5 pieces of high value-added content.

- Create anticipation and a high level of interest.

- Close the launch at a specific date to instigate scarcity (in an internet startup this could be similar to launching to a restricted set of users).

- Let the press or other internet venues talk about your product to help create anticipation.

- Create revenue share alliances with influencers and distributors so that the launch outreach is maximized (there are a lot of details and considerations on this point).

Paolo Messina and Michael Fox

Driving, Informing or Collaborating with Marketing

Context:

There are at least two situations where product managers' work is intertwined with marketing. One is the growth hacking team which is typical of internet companies and/or the digital product components from companies in other industries. The second situation is the very early stage startups. In this latter case product managers can drive digital marketing. Today social media marketing and growth hacking are utilized in a variety of products and services. In startups they are also used to raise capital. Product managers typically inform product marketers about features etc. but anything from targeting, positioning, lead generation and sales material is owned by product marketers. More B2B tips will follow in the next section.

84 The more knowledge of the end customer you have, the better you can target the ads. Precision in describing the opportunity or pain point goes a long way.

85 Communication in any form should be value-driven. That is, your marketing communication should start partly in education and partly in shedding light on a potential solution for your customer's problem.

86 The complexity of the product and the maturity of the market has a huge impact on your spending, regardless of which platform you pick: social, display, search or other channels. If the product is complex you will have to create awareness.

87 In the latter case, you need to have the patience to stage the marketing. First, create problem awareness, then solution awareness, then your solution awareness, and finally desire and vision. Vision drives the sales. This is very easy to understand and extremely difficult to put into practice. The number of marketing stages necessary depends on how complex or expensive your product is and where the prospective customer is in terms of awareness and how much pain the prospect is currently experiencing.

88 If you work for a company that has a sufficient budget, you need to optimize your market for customer lifetime value.

In startups, especially at the beginning, this is not always possible, so the economics of conversion take a premier position in driving marketing expenditure.

89 Decision science and visuals can be used to decrease your customer acquisition cost. However, this approach can backfire as often using too much of a design and nice graphics can attract curious individuals instead of genuine prospects with a problem you can solve. Classic advertising books warn about this problem.

90 Programmatic and digital advertising are very common today, but there are other ways to generate customers and leads. This includes prospecting techniques and growth hacking techniques, among others.

91 Be prepared to invest in acquiring marketing data from a major platform. You can do some research, but many questions, including which platform is better to use first, will best be answered with experiments (and experiments cost money). You can find more info in the growth hacking community for B2C products and content marketing/lead generation for B2B products.

92 Most platforms use algorithms, most likely a combination of unsupervised and supervised learning, to display the correct ad in front of the potential best customers. It takes some time before they get the algorithm (and time means money). If you prefer, there is a price to pay for calibrating the algorithm aspects of the digital platform you use.

93 You must analyze your results in great detail. This is especially true with complex ad bidding platforms such as Google Adwords. This platform has virtually thousands of settings, and it can give the illusion that campaigns are working well, until you find out your ad is being displayed in Iran[6] and it is converting like crazy.

---

[6] At the time of this writing this is a known Google ad issue that is reported in various blogs. Usually the company doesn't charge for advertising displayed in countries you had not selected.

Special Considerations for B2B Products

Context:

Product managers in B2B companies, including service companies, may work on providing customized solutions or may have to equip their products to integrate into enterprise workflows. Here we offer some special tips.

94 In B2B, a portion of the company's revenue may come from building solutions. Even if the company has a Software-as-a-Service model, the largest customers require a Proof-of-Concept (POC). Depending on the company, a product manager may work on the POC or not. In the event you do, here are few schematic hints:

- Discover the set of decision makers and who the ultimate customer is.

- Diagnose the complex problem companies in your customer's industry face in detail.

- Design a value-rich solution that decommoditizes your position.

- Deliver the value with strong execution.

95 In a previous point, we mentioned that sales engineers are resources for customer and product research. The opposite is also true. Because they look at the specific sale, sometimes they end up putting pressure on product management to create customized (or on/off) solutions that have little value for the company in the long term. You should analyze the pros and cons in this situation and deny any features that do not serve a long term objective (limitations do apply: if the sales and sales engineering teams are closing a $1B contract that is a long term value in itself!).

96 B2B products may require a higher complexity in the feature set. Usually multiple product managers work on various elements of the product offering. However, we recommend having a clear understanding of the deployment environment and how the product feature set should be designed. Here is a list of the most salient additional features:

- Check and satisfy Customer network and security requirements

- Check and satisfy Customer computation and processing limitations or requirements

- Satisfy hierarchy of users' role within the customer organization

- Offering the ability to monitor performances and a rich set of analytic insights

- Understanding customer's data storage requirements and limitations

- Understanding customer data privacy priorities and specific issues

Special Considerations for B2C Products

Context:

For product managers that work in consumers companies, understanding consumer behaviour is a great plus. This is a highly researched area in psychology, behavioral science and marketing. Here is an extract of specialized tips for the monetization of these digital and physical products:

97 Use these three drivers to consumer purchases to design the monetization experience:

- Desire: " I really want it...I am salivating..."

- Vision: "What will happen to me if I buy this... this is how I see myself ..."

- Belief: "I believe this brand is not good...I believe this product is good but not for me..."

98 Belief is determined by at least three of our mental biases, and here is what can be done to help people overcome negative beliefs about your product :

- Habit bias: Advertise to people at a point of change or to people that are likely to experience a change in life.

- Priming effect: Avoid missteps during launch. Otherwise, it will be difficult to change people's beliefs.

- Confirmation bias: People interpret reality in view of their beliefs and previous experiences. Try to use subtle product features to affect their subconscious without eliciting a conscious reaction.

99 Expectancy theory is the idea that we experience what we expect. Here are the consequences:

- Superb packaging contributes to product sales and product acceptance (see Apple delightful packaging).

- Price can affect perception of quality. Discounting can be tricky in some product categories.

100 Social proof: Many customers are loving it, the most loved in a certain category. In most situations, indicating that the product is successfully used by many others is a way to increase adoption. Number of customer reviews is a big driver for many products.

101 Negative social proof: Avoid saying things like, "If more customers bought it we could charge only $5." You are telling people that not many people buy it, so people you say this to will not buy it! Copy is very important in internet and packaged products. Be aware of this impact.

Bonus Tip! The user context affects behaviour significantly. An example: "I listen to Spotify when I am trying to get motivated at the gym. There is no chance I will watch the video ad that Spotify shows me every 30 minutes as my phone is wrapped on my arm. Also, 30 seconds interruption is too long. If Spotify injected 10 second audio ads about a great marketing book I should read next, it probably would get my attention because I can tolerate 10 seconds interruption in this situation, and I am very eager to learn about new books." Try to analyze the context in which a product is used and how you could improve design and marketing to account for people in context.

Manufactured by Amazon.ca
Acheson, AB

11393874R00048